SIXTH TRAINING GROUP
30 Immoral Security Failings and Corrective Best Practices Guidebook, with a Statement on a Conversation Related to Written Policy

Published and Distributed by
SIXTH TRAINING GROUP
matthewsmith7377@gmail.com

© 2019 by Matthew Smith
ISBN 9781091881259

First Printing: March 2019

SIXTH TRAINING GROUP
30 Immoral Security Failings and Corrective Best Practices Guidebook, with a Statement on a Conversation Related to Written Policy

BY
MATTHEW SMITH

FOR USE WITH
Sixth Training Group
Security Operations Desk Blotter

RECOMMENDED TRAINING STANDARDS FOR PERSONNEL:
Ethical Protection Standards for Personnel Involved in Security Operations, Individual Training Requirements, 2019 Edition
ITR 1000.19.A

SIXTH TRAINING GROUP

CONTENTS:

A. ABOUT THE GUIDEBOOK

In the operations of the current security industry, attempts to maximize profits have replaced ethical priorities. Instead of seeking security personnel who exemplify high standards of performance, the industry leadership has sought the lowest standard of performance in order to undercut competitors with similarly low standards, creating a downward race toward a supposedly acceptable minimum. In the author's experience, performance has fallen significantly below an acceptable level, and the result is a web of unethical behavior from industry leadership which seeks to conceal performance failures.

In typical security operations, lip service is paid to performing excellent service, yet little to no effort is devoted to ethical evaluation of procedures and practices. Current industry leadership does not hold personnel accountable to understand that actions may have ethical consequences, and allows persons to continue in positions of responsibility even after proven ethical failures. In a security operation which is led in an ethical manner, a high priority will be assigned to evaluating practices and procedures, and to implementing practices which are ethical and biblical.

It is the mission of Sixth Training Group to present an ethical alternative to the failures of the current security industry. To that end, the author has prepared a guidebook which relates current practices which are deficient, and proposes corrective measures which are ethical, and which promote high, standardized performance.

B. GUIDEBOOK INTENT

The Immoral Security Failings and Corrective Best Practices Guidebook (referred to as "the guidebook") is intended to serve as an aid for personnel engaged in security operations, by providing examples of failed, flawed, and unethical practices with corrective policies, procedures, and practices, or order to facilitate ethical behavior and high performance. Use of the guidebook for any other purpose constitutes misuse. The author and Sixth Training Group accept no liability resulting from the use or misuse of the guidebook. Use of the guidebook is subject to the terms of the Sixth Training Group 'Security-Related Written Materials Agreement,' and use of the guidebook for any purpose implies acceptance of those terms.

The final responsibility for all security operations and for the content of all security-related reports rests with the personnel conducting the operations. Sixth Training Group recommends a minimum of 12 weeks of thorough training in all aspects of security operations before personnel are given responsibility for security operations. Use of the guidebook is not a substitute for adequate training. **PERFORMANCE OF SECURITY OPERATIONS BY INADEQUATELY TRAINED PERSONNEL, OR BY PERSONNEL WHOSE PERFORMANCE IS INADEQUATE, CREATES AN INCREASED RISK OF DEATH OR SERIOUS BODILY INJURY.**

C. SECURITY-RELATED WRITTEN MATERIALS AGREEMENT

I. Statement of Intent

The security-related written materials including, but not limited to, Individual Training Requirements, Security Operations Desk Blotter, Security Operations Communication Log, Event Report, Facility Status Report, Equipment Status Report, Desk Blotter Handbook, and Standardized Bomb Threat Supplement (referred to as "the materials") produced by the authors (collectively referred to as "Sixth Training Group"), and distributed by Sixth Training Group, are intended to provide guidance for security leaders, by providing information on security best practices, in order to facilitate ethical behavior and high performance when conducting security operations. Use of the materials for any purpose other than those expressed in this agreement constitutes misuse. Sixth Training Group accepts no liability resulting from the use or misuse of the materials. Use of the materials is subject to the terms of this agreement. By using the materials, any person, business, or other entity agrees to accept all parts of this agreement.

II. Responsibility for Operations

The final responsibility for all security operations, including responsibility for the content of all security-related reports, rests with the personnel conducting the operations. Sixth Training Group does not assume any responsibility related to conducting security operations for any entity. Any person, business, or other entity who uses the materials agrees to assume all responsibility for conducting security operations, including any burden to ensure legal or regulatory compliance, and agrees to assume all legal, financial, or other consequences resulting from security-related failures. Any person, business, or other entity who uses the materials agrees to assume all responsibility for the content of security-related reports, including, but not limited to, their clarity, their accuracy, their completeness, and their safekeeping, including any burden to ensure legal or regulatory compliance, and agrees to assume all legal, financial, or other consequences resulting from security-related failures.

III. Responsibility for Training

The final responsibility for the training of all personnel, including personnel performance assessment, rests with the personnel leading security operations. Through distribution of the materials, Sixth Training Group does not assume any responsibility related to training personnel on behalf of any entity. Any person, business, or other entity who uses the materials agrees to assume all responsibility for training personnel, including any burden to ensure legal or regulatory compliance, and agrees to assume all

legal, financial, or other consequences resulting from failure to ensure adequate training. Sixth Training Group recommends a minimum of 12 weeks of thorough training in all aspects of security operations before personnel are given responsibility for security operations.
PERFORMANCE OF SECURITY OPERATIONS BY INADEQUATELY TRAINED PERSONNEL, OR BY PERSONNEL WHOSE PERFORMANCE IS INADEQUATE, CREATES AN INCREASED RISK OF DEATH OR SERIOUS BODILY INJURY.

IV. The Materials Not Legal Advice

The materials provided by Sixth Training Group are not intended to be legal advice, or represented to be a substitute for legal advice. Sixth Training Group does not assume any responsibility related to ensuring the legal status of the operations of any entity. Any person, business, or other entity who uses the materials agrees to consult with counsel as required, and agrees to assume all legal, financial, or other consequences resulting from failure to consult with counsel.

V. Errors and Omissions in the Materials

The materials provided by Sixth Training Group are intended to be highly accurate. The materials may contain minor inaccuracies, omissions, or typographical errors. Any person, business, or other entity who uses the materials agrees that Sixth Training Group is not responsible for such errors, and agrees to assume any legal, financial, or other consequences which may result from inaccurate security-related reports.

VI. The Materials Include No Guarantees

Sixth Training Group provides no guarantees of any outcome or result to follow from the use of the materials. Any person, business, or other entity who uses the materials agrees that outcome will depend solely on the performance of personnel who lead and conduct security operations for that entity.

VII. The Materials Include No Warranties

SIXTH TRAINING GROUP PROVIDES THE MATERIALS 'AS IS' WITHOUT WARRANTY OF ANY KIND. WARRANTY OR REPRESENTATION OF FITNESS FOR A PARTICULAR PURPOSE IS EXPRESSLY DISCLAIMED. ANY PERSON, BUSINESS, OR OTHER ENTITY WHO USES THE MATERIALS AGREES TO ACCEPT THE MATERIALS WITHOUT WARRANTY OF ANY KIND.

VIII. Assumption of Risk

Sixth Training Group provides no assurance that use of the materials will be free from risk. Any person, business, or other entity who uses the materials agrees to assume all risk, including legal, financial, or other consequences, which result from any unknown risks or unforeseen risks.

IX. Limitation of Liability

Any person, business, or other entity who uses the materials agrees to absolve Sixth Training Group (including the authors and all persons associated with Sixth Training Group) of any loss, liability, or other adverse consequences which may result from the use of the materials. Any person, business, or other entity who uses the materials agrees that Sixth Training Group will not be liable to that entity, or to any other entity, for any type of loss or damages resulting from use of the materials.

X. Indemnification and Release

Any person, business, or other entity who uses the materials agrees to fully and completely defend, hold harmless, indemnify, and release Sixth Training Group (including the authors and all persons associated with Sixth Training Group) from any and all causes of action, allegations, suits, claims, damages, or demands that result from use of the materials, or are in any way related to the materials.

Additional copies of the 'Security-Related Written Materials Agreement' can be obtained by contacting Sixth Training Group.

MATTHEW SMITH

Immoral Security Practice #1: Failure to acknowledge Christ's authority, which requires applying the Sixth Commandment to security operations

Ethical business practices must acknowledge the Lordship of Christ over everything which they do, and must accept the authority of the Bible to set or correct their professional standards. This requires security operations to be directed to the goal of applying the Sixth Commandment, which demands appropriate protection of lives and appropriate use of force at all times. If a security company fails to view the profession as a calling and responsibility before God, all of their efforts will be misdirected.

Best practices for security operations should demand that all leadership personnel make a commitment to professional standards which apply the Sixth Commandment, and to ingrain the protection of lives as an individual responsibility belonging to every person in the profession. The professional commitment must specify that all policy will contain priorities, procedures, and practices which support these goals. Lack of commitment in this area should be regarded as disqualifying for security leadership.

Immoral Security Practice #2: Deification of money

If the management of security a company views security operations as merely business operations, it will require security staff to advance the goals set by the business. If the foremost goals of a security company are (1A) to provide the cheapest service possible in order to maximize profits, and (2A) to reduce company liability as much as possible in order to maximize profits, then they are failing in the goals which should be foremost, namely, (1B) to protect personnel as effectively as possible in order to prevent loss of life, (2B) to provide a cost-effective service in order to protect as many people as feasible. Goals 1A and 2A are idolatrous, and must be exposed as deification of money.

Best practices for security operations should demand that all leadership personnel must demonstrate at all times a high degree of dedication to protecting personnel. Lack of commitment in this area should be regarded as disqualifying for security leadership.

Immoral Security Practice #3: Lack of written professional standards

If the management of a security company fails to implement written professional standards, they are demonstrating a lack of leadership. A key feature of genuine leadership is willingness to train in accordance with a defined standard. This means clear written guidelines for performance, specifying tasks to be performed, with a time and a standard required to be met for each task. Written policy must also explain the intent behind each task, and explain how the task accomplishes the professional goal. Stating intent is critical, so that initiative is not crushed by rote performance. When these kinds of standards are not a high priority for leaders, an organization will lack direction and professionalism.

Best practices for security operations should demand that all leadership personnel must provide written performance standards for all tasks their subordinates are expected to perform. If standards do not exist, leaders must be capable of defining a reasonable level of performance, and must write and distribute that standard.

Immoral Security Practice #4: Unwillingness to hold personnel accountable

If the management of a security company fails to hold personnel accountable to understand responsibilities and to perform tasks to standard, they are demonstrating a lack of leadership. Security supervisors should regularly engage in point-by-point discussion of post orders with the personnel they are required to supervise in order to ensure comprehension. Supervisors should regularly require demonstration of ability to perform all critical emergency tasks.

Best practices for security operations should demand that all leadership personnel must verify that competency of subordinate personnel in all required tasks. Lack of commitment in this area should be regarded as disqualifying for security leadership.

Immoral Security Practice #5: Retaining and promoting incompetent personnel

Individuals who fail at basic tasks – such as failing to account for equipment, failing to follow identification verification policy, or failing to keep facility doors locked – should never be trusted with responsibility for the lives and safety of others. If the management of a security company fails to hold incompetent personnel accountable to perform these tasks with excellence, they inevitably will eventually entrust leadership to individuals who disregard their responsibilities. If these failings are concealed, and these individuals continue in career advancement, then an organization is one generation away from professional collapse.

Best practices for security operations should demand that all personnel undergo regular performance assessments, and that all failures in assessments and in actual events be consistently documented. Individuals who do not demonstrate consistently high performance and dedication to professional duties should not continue to be entrusted with positions of responsibility.

Immoral Security Practice #6: Displaying symbols of violence and death in the workplace

Deadly force is appropriately used only defensively when people are in imminent danger of death or serious bodily harm, and even then only as a last resort when lesser means have failed or cannot reasonably be employed. If the personnel of security companies display images of skulls or of individuals swinging swords in the workplace, it undermines what should be a strong commitment to the appropriate use of force by security personnel. Having all or part of a dead body on display in the workplace, outside of a defensive context, exhibits a fascination with violence, and suggests disregard for human life. Similarly, having a weapon on displayed in the workplace, outside of a defensive context, exhibits a fascination with inflicting deadly force, and suggests an intent to intimidate with threat of violence.

Best practices for security operations should require that no depiction of all or part of an injured or dead human being be displayed on the premises. It should also be required that no depiction of any weapon, except a weapon authorized for defensive use at the premises, be displayed on the premises, and that any depiction of a weapon must show use of appropriate safety practices.

Immoral Security Practice #7: Unclear or concealed policy intent

Besides applying all the implications of the Sixth Commandment, the next critical responsibility in security operations is applying the Ninth Commandment. If clear intent is not provided with all instructions, then the truth is concealed in equivocation, reducing the ability of personnel to determine appropriate action. "To protect property," "to prevent workplace accidents," or "to protect personnel," are examples of statements of intent. If security staff are told to turn on certain lights at certain times, but not informed of intent, then it is left unclear how to react to burned out bulbs, for instance. If the intent provided is "to prevent concealment of an intruder," or "to provide an illuminated walk path during hours of operation," then intent is clarified and correct action can be determined.

Best practices for security operations should demand that all instructions have accompanying intent. Instructions are not considered to be delivered until a brief-back is received from the subordinate which correctly states the intent of the instruction.

Immoral Security Practice #8: Improper policy intent

Unclear or concealed intent is not the only intent-related problem in security operations. The more serious problem is incorrect expressions of intent. Security policy commonly cites a top-level intent such as "in order to deter crime," or "to protect property." The problem with these expressions is that they are immoral, since the only proper top-level intent is "to protect personnel"; any benefits of crime-reduction, property protection, or continuing business operations must be a secondary concern, considered after protection of personnel. Similarly, an emergency manual might say that the goal is for security staff to call 911 in order to get emergency personnel on site. The proper goal, though, is to protect lives. Often this means prioritizing a 911 call, but sometimes it means closing and locking a door, or barricading a window. The point here is that security personnel should never be required to violate policy in order to perform their responsibilities – that kind of policy is always immoral.

Best practices for security operations should demand that all instructions have accompanying intent. Instructions are not considered to be delivered until a brief-back is received from the subordinate which correctly states the intent of the instruction.

Immoral Security Practice #9: Uncommunicative leadership

The Ninth Commandment does not merely require a technical, narrow avoidance of falsehoods, it requires clear communication and forbids improper silence. If the management of a security company fails to communicate performance expectations, including guidance on how performance will be measured, it is not only an effective way to guarantee failure, it is disregard for the truth – this is especially true at the supervision level: if a supervisor does not verbally confirm understanding of a written instruction with a brief-back of the intent, the supervisor is failing in an essential responsibility.

Best practices for security operations should demand that all instructions are propagated in formal briefings or by written instructions which follow a consistent format; all personnel must have an opportunity to assess their understanding of the policy or procedure with leadership personnel. Personnel who fail to confirm the comprehension of written instructions by subordinates should be regarded as disqualified for security leadership.

Immoral Security Practice #10: Incomplete written instructions

Transmitting incomplete written instructions also displays rejection of the truth. Many organizations and governments create their written policies from generic templates. I have seen deadly force policies which inconsistently mixed standard numerals 1, 2, 3, etc. with Roman numerals I, II, III, etc. and letters A, B, C, etc. I have seen emergency manuals with sections marked "insert information here" with no text inserted. This clearly shows lack of commitment from leadership to support subordinate personnel. It is even more deceptive if the organization claims to provide written guidance.

Best practices for security operations should demand a high level of accuracy, clarity, and correct format and organization in all written policies. Personnel who propagate incomplete templates as written policy should be regarded as disqualified for security leadership.

Immoral Security Practice #11: Verbal instructions contrary to written policy

The natural culmination of disregard for the truth is to transmit verbal instructions contrary to written instructions. It is common that a handbook of written policy be formally enacted, but then effectively ignored in favor of practices more convenient to implement. This practice can be advantageous for some companies, because it allows them to have a strict procedure on paper, while they can plead ignorance of lax practices. At the same time, security staff may be pressured to follow the lax procedure. This is deception and misrepresentation at several levels, (1) it misrepresents expectations to security staff, (2) it deceives clients and auditors of what policy is actually performed, and (3) it lays the foundation for an unethical legal defense against liabilities incurred if the lax procedure leads to loss of life.

Best practices for security operations should demand uniformity between written policy and verbal instructions. Propagation of verbal instructions contrary to written policy should result in immediate disqualification from further security operations.

Immoral Security Practice #12: Confusing assortment of reporting methods

If the management of a security company does not have a clear chain of creating reports, reviewing and distributing reports, preserving reports, and auditing reports, they are undermining the truth. It is common that a post might have as many as six different ways of reporting information – such as daily logs, undated notebooks, verbal reports, event reports, electronic reports, and e-mailed reports – while providing minimal guidelines for which methods to use in different circumstances. Further, if information is reported, but supervision does not acknowledge in writing the receipt of the information, then the reports can easily be destroyed by supervision with no record preserved.

Best practices for security operations should demand that the desk blotter for every shift or tour will include a summation of any report, including the type of report, and the number of pages if applicable. When a report is received, there should be a reviewable verification with the supervisor's signature on the desk blotter, including a record of report distribution and storage or preservation if applicable. Failure to properly distribute or preserve reports should result in immediate disqualification from further security operations.

Immoral Security Practice #13: Failure to implement procedure for access during non-business hours

Personnel are placed at increased risk of violent attack if the management of a security company does not have a clear policy for allowing access to facilities during non-business hours. If a facility had a policy for all doors to be secured during non-business hours, and if the policy required security staff never to expose themselves to risk, and then unknown individuals arrived at the facility, then it would be a violation of policy to open the door to let such a person have access to the facility. If this were a situation where verbal instructions had been given that security staff must open the door, it would create a dilemma because of the immoral leadership.

Best practices for security operations should demand that during non-business hours, any building access must be cleared by a telephone call to security staff. The person attempting entry must provide full name and reason for entering. Security staff must have time to check records for a photos or credentials, verify whether the person still works at the facility, and to obtain third-party authorization if required. Failure to implement a policy for access during non-business hours should be regarded as disqualifying for security leadership. Attempt to implement an access policy contrary to written policy should result in immediate disqualification from further security operations.

Immoral Security Practice #14: Disregarding written policy

If the management of a security company allows violations of written policy related to facility access, it places personnel at increased risk of violent attack. If written policy requires entries to remain locked, and to be closed except when in use, in order to prevent unauthorized entry, then unlocking them for mere convenience would be a serious breach of professional ethics.

Best practices for security operations should demand that security staff must demonstrate at all times a high level of dedication to keeping the premises secure. Intentional neglect of precautions related to facility access should result in immediate disqualification from further security operations. Personnel who fail to hold all security staff accountable to this standard should be regarded as disqualified for security leadership.

Immoral Security Practice #15: Concealing security vulnerabilities

If the management of a security company conceals reports of disqualifying behavior, it demonstrates (1) disregard for the responsibility to protect human lives, and (2) disregard for the responsibility to be truthful to client and customers. Normally, security supervisors and management do not gain financially from client companies being aware of security risks; rather, they gain from continuing business as usual. As a result, damaging information may be frequently suppressed, and personnel who should be disqualified from positions of trust, are simply moved to other sites, all at the expense of increase risk to people.

Best practices for security operations should demand that all identified security vulnerabilities – including risks caused by security staff neglect – be openly and honestly reported to clients. Lack of commitment in this area should be regarded as disqualifying for security leadership.

Immoral Security Practice #16: Belief that massacres cannot be stopped

If a security company allows security supervisors to instruct security staff that nothing can be done to stop armed perpetrators of massacres, provides 'Run, Hide, Fight' presentations to security staff, leads them believe that the best course of action is to run away at the first sign of danger, and refuses to implement an emergency plan for the event of an active killer, these actions increase the risk of a massacre.

Best practices for security operations should demand that an emergency plan is implemented envisioning an attack by an active killer. Instead of ineffective 'Run, Hide, Fight' measures, security staff should be required to have means to use appropriate force. Spreading the belief that massacres cannot be stopped should result in immediate disqualification from further security operations.

Immoral Security Practice #17: Neglecting the essential elements of vigilance

If a security company allows security staff to neglect the essential elements of vigilance by playing computer games and watching TV shows during periods when they should be conducting situation assessment, standardized observation techniques, and behavioral profiling, it reveals a lack of dedication to protecting human lives by company leadership.

Best practices for security operations should demand that security staff will demonstrate at all times a high level of dedication to the responsibility of protecting human lives. Any activity which prevents security staff from remaining vigilant will not be permitted. Demonstrated lack of commitment to vigilance should result in immediate disqualification from further security operations.

Immoral Security Practice #18: Failure to provide relevant training

All members of security staff should have training relevant to the risks expected. For example, when expecting threats by ex-employees made against supervisors, and threats made by stalkers or abusive family members against employees, security staff should receive training to verbally diffuse or deescalate potentially violent confrontations, such as the courses available from the Verbal Judo Institute. This training would need to be accompanied by simulations where an individual would role-play by delivering verbal abuse or physical threats, and security staff would be required to demonstrate ability to remain calm under stress and to continue to accomplish the professional goal. If a security company fails to provide this kind of focused, risk-specific training, it demonstrates a lack of commitment to protecting human lives.

Best practices for security operations should require a risk assessment matrix to be completed for any facility with posted security staff. There must be relevant training assigned for every risk where security staff is given responsibility, and policy must include a written justification for why the provided training is relevant and is adequate. At minimum, training should cover the areas of verbal mastery, emergency task performance, situation assessment, standardized observation techniques, behavioral profiling, and violence prevention. Lack of commitment to providing relevant training should be regarded as disqualifying for security leadership.

Immoral Security Practice #19: Failure to prepare, practice, and drill emergency tasks

It is imperative that all security staff can place emergency calls with primary systems and backup systems, can operate emergency alert systems, including fire and tornado alarms, can perform bomb threat procedure, and other site-specific emergency tasks. Ability to perform each of these tasks in a timely, successful manner should be demonstrated periodically. If a security company fails to perform all of this, including regular drills on all emergency tasks, it demonstrates a lack of commitment to protecting human lives. Earlier, an example was provided that sometimes entries and windows might need to be secured before placing a 911 call. It is imperative that in any sort of emergency, situation assessment must be the first step, so that the next correct action is taken, in order to protect lives.

Best practices for security operations should demand that drills of all emergency tasks are regularly performed, with performance documented. Inadequate performance in any task should be addressed with relevant training in a timely manner, and adequate performance must be subsequently documented. Lack of commitment to performing regular emergency drills should be regarded as disqualifying for security leadership.

Immoral Security Practice #20: Failure to standardize a floor plan and terminology

If the management of a security company does not provide a standardized facility floor plan, does not make efforts to use standardized terminology, and does not prepare in advance for emergency responders to utilize the floor plan and be able to communicate seamlessly with security staff, then security operations are being designed to fail, and lack of commitment to protecting human lives is demonstrated.

Best practices for security operations should demand that facility management provide a standardized floor plan and arrange for the use of standardized terminology. Preparations should be made in advance for communication with emergency responders in a situation where their movements might need to be directed by security staff.

Immoral Security Practice #21: Lack of Preparation for Emergency Events.

If the management of a security company promotes a 'run, hide, fight' emergency plan, without making an effort to identify and prepare locations of adequate cover and concealment, it demonstrates a lack of commitment to protecting human lives.

Best practices for security operations should demand that any emergency plan be accompanied by a comprehensive facility assessment and physical inspection, envisioning the practical application of the plan, and policy must include a written justification for why lock-down areas and evacuation routes are adequate.

Immoral Security Practice #22: Failure to implement a program for reporting security risks

If the management of a security company fails to implement a transparent program for reporting security risks, risk is increased that risks will remain unaddressed over an extended period of time.

Best practices for security operations should demand that any reported risk have a timely assessment performed by security leadership, and feedback must be provided so that all personnel are informed of the intent of leadership, and all personnel are aware of implemented mitigation efforts, in order to enable all security staff to continue to assess ongoing risks.

Immoral Security Practice #23: Lack of relevant support

If the management of a security company fails to provide security staff with photos or descriptions of terminated employees, fails to fully inform security staff of relevant details regarding threats of violence issued by ex-employees, stalkers, or abusive family members, or fails to keep all emergency contact information updated, risk is increased, and lack of commitment to protecting human lives is demonstrated.

Best practices for security operations should demand that all emergency contact information is regularly reviewed. All personnel, including client personnel, contractors, and sub-contractors, should be informed that it is critical that security staff be informed of any relevant changes.

Immoral Security Practice #24: Bad camera views

If the management of a security company allows the placement of observation cameras in a manner that allows blind spots, restricted fields of view, or other limitations on visibility, it severely increases risk and reduces the ability of security staff to remain aware of the current situation.

Best practices for security operations should demand that all cameras which are relied upon for observation should be regularly inspected and evaluated, considering placement and quality of image. Limitations on visibility should be reported in the standard risk-reporting procedure, and should be resolved in a timely manner.

Immoral Security Practice #25: Sleep deprivation

If the management of a security company allows security staff to be on duty while severely sleep-deprived, it should be regarded in the same manner as if management were allowing individuals to be on duty while intoxicated. The impairment from lack of sleep lowers nearly all areas of mental and fine motor performance, and severely increases risk.

Best practices for security operations should be to require an 8-hour sleep opportunity prior to commencing a duty period, and requiring that no regular duty period may exceed 10.5 hours. Appropriate exceptions may be made only in cases of emergency. Written justification must be provided by leadership, showing why, in the case in question, it was reasonable to allow sleep deprivation.

Immoral Security Practice #26: Carelessness in accounting for keys and access badges

Security staff should be required to preserve a proper record when distributing, should properly safeguard facility keys at all times, and should account for all keys and access badges at the end of every shift. If the management of a security company does not hold security staff accountable in all of these areas, risk is seriously increased that unauthorized access could be gained to the facility.

Best practices for security operations should demand that all keys and all access badges be accounted for at the end of every shift. Any key or badge distributed must have a proper record preserved, which is verified at the end of the shift if the item has not yet been returned. The safekeeping of keys and access badges must be reviewed periodically, with performance concerns documented and addressed. All security personnel must be required to demonstrate commitment at all times to the safekeeping of keys and access badges; lack of commitment in this area should be regarded as disqualifying.

Immoral Security Practice #27: Failure to standardize contact procedures

If the management of a security company fails to standardize procedures for dealing with high-risk groups (e.g., terminated employees, individuals with a restraining order), risk of a violent attack is increased. Without a standardized procedure in place, the manner in which these volatile situations are handled will vary based on the skill, alertness, and mood of whoever happens to be on duty.

Best practices for security operations should be to require a standardized procedure for dealing with any high-risk individual, or any unknown individual. The best procedure is probably the five step procedure taught by The Verbal Judo Institute. An alternate procedure could be the 5 As: Address with respect, Ask to leave, Advise they are trespassing, Alert management, and Act to secure premises. In the 5 As, 911 is called at any point where appropriate, and the security staff advances to the 5th step at any point where appropriate. Whatever procedure is used, every member of the security staff should have the entire procedure memorized, know the reason for every step, and be able to give examples of the conditions for calling 911 or for advancing to the 5th step.

Immoral Security Practice #28: Disarming Security Staff

It is an ethical and legal principle that deadly force cannot be used to protect property, and can only be used to protect people from imminent threat of death or serious injury. If a company attempts to prevent possession of firearms – which are the appropriate means of using deadly force to protect human life against violent attack – that company is creating a situation where deadly force cannot be used to protect people. This policy effectively reduces personnel to the level of mere property, and enables murderers to more effectively kill security staff and other personnel.

Best practices for security operations should require that any security staff with a protective responsibility are required to possess the means of deadly force at all times. Demonstrated attempts to prevent possession of the means of deadly force should result in immediate disqualification from further security operations.

Immoral Security Practice #29: Denying Security Staff Lesser Means of Defense

Often the same companies that attempt to prevent the possession of firearms also attempt to prevent the possession of any lesser means to protect lives, even significantly less effective means, such as O/C sprays, electrical devices, or body armor. This policy clearly reduces the ability of security staff to survive any violent attack, and reduces their ability to delay, hinder, or stop any person intending to commit a massacre. This policy places security staff and other personnel at increased risk of death or serious bodily harm.

Best practices for security operations should demand that security staff are given access to an appropriate array of defensive equipment, and are supported with relevant training. Any policy which forbids the possession of equipment must either, (1) reasonably demonstrate that the equipment has no legitimate use for defensive purposes, or (2) reasonably demonstrate that the equipment has serious drawbacks not possessed by readily available substitutes. Demonstrated attempts to prevent the possession of effective defensive equipment should result in immediate disqualification from further security operations.

Immoral Security Practice #30: Enforcing Disarmament Policies

Often the same companies that implement disarmament policies also attempt to enlist security staff to enforce disarmament policies upon others. This sort of policy represents the complete perversion of what should be the proper intent of security operations, to protect personnel, and replaces it with practices which would make security staff the enablers of murderers.

Best practices for security operations should demand that security personnel make a professional commitment to never engage in disarmament efforts. Demonstrated attempts to deny to others the appropriate means of deadly force should result in immediate disqualification from further security operations.

Annex A: Statement on a Conversation Related to Written Policy

I recently had a conversation with a corporate-level executive of a security company. I asked him to give me his thoughts on verbal instructions that exceeded the boundaries set out in written policy or that went counter to written policy.

This was his response: "Because of fluctuations and the changes in the environment, the verbal order becomes the policy, if you will. It's not necessarily the best way of going about it, and not necessarily something that's in concrete. If in fact a supervisor, or a lead, or someone in authority tells you 'this is what the policy is at this time,' then you have to take that kind of as is. And to expect a written policy on all issues, it oftentimes becomes difficult form various standpoints. The policy could change, and maybe that's one of the reasons they said what they said. Noticing that with any type of situation where we have a client who may be kind of on the fence, we won't post an official policy in writing, we'll just say to the client, 'fine, this is what the policy will be for now,' we would like to keep talking about this and see if we can change this policy, for whatever reason, and just go forward from there. Obviously, we're in constant contact with the client to see what they want, and what they prefer."

His argument seems to be that it would be counterproductive to write down a policy which is subject to change or future revision. However, this is an excuse made on behalf of a failed and unethical system, not a position founded on best practices learned from experience. In actual experience, this system has many problems, including, (1) a verbal instruction is likely to be relayed from supervisor, to night shift, to morning shift, to weekend shift, so that once an instruction is received neither its authority or content is without question, (2) in this system, almost without exception, instructions will be relayed without accompanying intent, as mentioned in Immoral Security Practice #7, which means that the goal of the policy is not able to be performed except under ideal conditions, (3) in this system, written instructions will continue to be propagated and used for training years after they are outdated, which effectively creates an official deception about what policy is current, and (4) once a web of verbal instructions disconnected from written policy are circulating, leaders no longer know what instructions have been relayed to whom, so they can no longer ensure performance or hold individuals accountable.

I have personally witnessed situations where the security staff and the maintenance department were working at cross-purposes, one group locking, and another unlocking the same door. This situation continued for weeks, because no leader was willing to write an email to all the people who had keys. It was finally resolved only when I conducted an investigation, discovered what was happening, and wrote an email to all parties concerned, where I wrote down the intent of the maintenance department, as it had been relayed to me, and stated that unless otherwise informed, I would follow that intent by keeping the door unlocked. One email fixed a situation where weeks of verbal instructions had failed.

The entire premise that a policy subject to change should not be written is *prima facie* ridiculous. The very best way to ensure that a policy is indeed able to be revised efficiently is to write it down! Writing the policy, and keeping a record of its distribution, ensures that the policy can be undone very efficiently. Writing the policy establishes the correct chain by which future revisions should be expected. Here's an example: "Client intent is that truck drivers would have access to the receiving lobby during all business hours. Going forward, security staff should unlock the exterior door about 5 minutes before posted business hours, and lock it about 10 minutes after business hours. If the department is continuing operations at the end of business hours, contact the department supervisor and follow instructions, because they are likely working overtime. Modifications to this policy will be distributed by the security supervisor. Current thinking is that the situation will be reevaluated in June." I fail to see how implementing this as written policy prevents flexibility, or rules out future changes.

Further, an ethical company will desire to apply the Ninth Commandment in all its operations. This requires the company communications to truth between individuals, and to avoid doubtful and equivocal statements. Writing down one policy, and then implementing another one by verbal instructions is not only bad business, it is wickedness.